MAX LUCADO

LIFE LESSONS *from*

JAMES

Practical Wisdom

PREPARED BY THE LIVINGSTONE CORPORATION

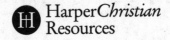

Harper*Christian*
Resources

Life Lessons from James
© 2018 by Max Lucado

Requests for information should be addressed to:
HarperChristian Resources, 3900 Sparks Dr. SE, Grand Rapids, Michigan 49546

ISBN 978-0-310-08660-4 (softcover)
ISBN 978-0-310-08661-1 (ebook)

HarperChristian Resources titles may be purchased in bulk for church, business, fundraising, or ministry use. For information, please e-mail ResourceSpecialist@ChurchSource.com.

Produced with the assistance of the Livingstone Corporation. Project staff include Jake Barton, Joel Bartlett, Andy Culbertson, Will Reaves, Mary Horner Collins, and Rachel Hawkins.

Editor: Len Woods

First Printing October 2018 / Printed in the United States of America

CONTENTS

HOW TO STUDY THE BIBLE

The Bible is a peculiar book. Words crafted in another language. Deeds done in a distant era. Events recorded in a far-off land. Counsel offered to a foreign people. It is a peculiar book.

It's surprising that anyone reads it. It's too old. Some of its writings date back 5,000 years. It's too bizarre. The book speaks of incredible floods, fires, earthquakes, and people with supernatural abilities. It's too radical. The Bible calls for undying devotion to a carpenter who called himself God's Son.

Logic says this book shouldn't survive. Too old, too bizarre, too radical.

The Bible has been banned, burned, scoffed, and ridiculed. Scholars have mocked it as foolish. Kings have branded it as illegal. A thousand times over the grave has been dug and the dirge has begun, but somehow the Bible never stays in the grave. Not only has it survived, but it has also thrived. It is the single most popular book in all of history. It has been the bestselling book in the world for years!

There is no way on earth to explain it. Which perhaps is the only explanation. For the Bible's durability is not found on *earth* but in *heaven*. The millions who have tested its claims and claimed its promises know there is but one answer: the Bible is God's book and God's voice.

As you read it, you would be wise to give some thought to two questions: *What is the purpose of the Bible?* and *How do I study the Bible?* Time spent reflecting on these two issues will greatly enhance your Bible study.

What is the purpose of the Bible?

Let the Bible itself answer that question: *"From infancy you have known the Holy Scriptures, which are able to make you wise for salvation through faith in Christ Jesus"* (2 Timothy 3:15).

The purpose of the Bible? Salvation. God's highest passion is to get his children home. His book, the Bible, describes his plan of salvation. The purpose of the Bible is to proclaim God's plan and passion to save his children.

This is the reason why this book has endured through the centuries. It dares to tackle the toughest questions about life: *Where do I go after I die? Is there a God? What do I do with my fears?* The Bible is the treasure map that leads to God's highest treasure—eternal life.

But how do you study the Bible? Countless copies of Scripture sit unread on bookshelves and nightstands simply because people don't know how to read it. What can you do to make the Bible real in your life?

The clearest answer is found in the words of Jesus: *"Ask and it will be given to you; seek and you will find; knock and the door will be opened to you"* (Matthew 7:7).

The first step in understanding the Bible is asking God to help you. You should read it prayerfully. If anyone understands God's Word, it is because of God and not the reader.

"The Advocate, the Holy Spirit, whom the Father will send in my name, will teach you all things and will remind you of everything I have said to you" (John 14:26).

Before reading the Bible, pray and invite God to speak to you. Don't go to Scripture looking for your idea, but go searching for his.

Not only should you read the Bible prayerfully, but you should also read it carefully. *"Seek and you will find"* is the pledge. The Bible is not a newspaper to be skimmed but rather a mine to be quarried. *"If you look for it as for silver and search for it as for hidden treasure, then you will understand the fear of the* LORD *and find the knowledge of God"* (Proverbs 2:4–5).

Any worthy find requires effort. The Bible is no exception. To understand the Bible, you don't have to be brilliant, but you must be willing to roll up your sleeves and search.

"Do your best to present yourself to God as one approved, a worker who does not need to be ashamed and who correctly handles the word of truth" (2 Timothy 2:15).

Here's a practical point. Study the Bible a bit at a time. Hunger is not satisfied by eating twenty-one meals in one sitting once a week. The body needs a steady diet to remain strong. So does the soul. When God sent food to his people in the wilderness, he didn't provide loaves already made. Instead, he sent them manna in the shape of *"thin flakes like frost on the ground"* (Exodus 16:14).

God gave manna in limited portions.

God sends spiritual food the same way. He opens the heavens with just enough nutrients for today's hunger. He provides *"a rule for this, a rule for that; a little here, a little there"* (Isaiah 28:10).

Don't be discouraged if your reading reaps a small harvest. Some days a lesser portion is all that is needed. What is important is to search every day for that day's message. A steady diet of God's Word over a lifetime builds a healthy soul and mind.

It's much like the little girl who returned from her first day at school feeling a bit dejected. Her mom asked, "Did you learn anything?"

"Apparently not enough," the girl responded. "I have to go back tomorrow, and the next day, and the next . . . "

Such is the case with learning. And such is the case with Bible study. Understanding comes little by little over a lifetime.

There is a third step in understanding the Bible. After the asking and seeking comes the knocking. After you ask and search, *"knock and the door will be opened to you"* (Matthew 7:7).

To knock is to stand at God's door. To make yourself available. To climb the steps, cross the porch, stand at the doorway, and volunteer. Knocking goes beyond the realm of thinking and into the realm of acting.

To knock is to ask, *What can I do? How can I obey? Where can I go?*

It's one thing to know what to do. It's another to do it. But for those who do it—those who choose to obey—a special reward awaits them.

"Whoever looks intently into the perfect law that gives freedom, and continues in it—not forgetting what they have heard, but doing it—they will be blessed in what they do" (James 1:25).

What a promise. Blessings come to those who do what they read in God's Word! It's the same with medicine. If you only read the label but ignore the pills, it won't help. It's the same with food. If you only read the recipe but never cook, you won't be fed. And it's the same with the Bible. If you only read the words but never obey, you'll never know the joy God has promised.

Ask. Search. Knock. Simple, isn't it? So why don't you give it a try? If you do, you'll see why the Bible is the most remarkable book in history.

H ere is a story James would have liked.

Francis of Assisi once invited an apprentice to go with him to a nearby village to preach. The young monk quickly agreed, seizing an opportunity to hear his teacher speak. When they arrived in the village, Francis began to visit with the people.

First he stopped in on the butcher. Next a visit with the cobbler. Then a short walk to the home of a woman who'd recently buried her husband. After that a stop at the school to chat with the teacher. This continued throughout the morning. After some time, Francis told his disciple that it was time to return to the abbey.

The student didn't understand. "But we came to preach," he reminded. "We haven't preached a sermon."

"Haven't we?" questioned the elder. "People have watched us, listened to us, responded to us. Every word we have spoken, every deed we have done has been a sermon. We have preached all morning."

James would have liked that. As far as he was concerned, Christianity was more action on Monday than worship on Sunday. "What good is it, my brothers and sisters, if someone claims to have faith but has no deeds? Can such faith save them?" (James 2:14).

His message is bare-knuckled. His style is bare-boned. Talk is cheap, he argues. Service is invaluable.

It's not that works *save* the Christian, but that works *mark* the Christian. In James's book of logic, it only makes sense that we who have been given much should give much. Not just with words. But with our lives.

Or, as St. Francis is noted as saying, "Preach without ceasing. If you must, use words."

James would have liked that too.

AUTHOR AND DATE

It is believed that James "the Just," the half-brother of Jesus and an influential leader in the early church, was the author of this short letter. James evidently did not initially believe Jesus was the promised Messiah (see John 7:5), but he changed his view when Jesus appeared to him after the resurrection (see 1 Corinthians 15:7). James rose to such prominence in the early church that he was recognized in standing alongside Peter and Paul. He played a key role in the Jerusalem Council, an early church debate as to whether non-Jews had to adopt Jewish practices in order to be considered Christians, ultimately ruling the church should "not make it difficult for the Gentiles who are turning to God" (Acts 15:19). James likely wrote the letter from Jerusalem c. AD 50, after the beginning of Paul and Barnabas's ministry in Antioch (see Acts 11:19–26) but prior to the events of the Jerusalem Council (see 15:1–21).

SITUATION

James addresses his letter to the "twelve tribes scattered among the nations" (1:1), which most likely refers to a group of Jewish Christians who were part of a general dispersion of Jews throughout the Mediterranean region (known as the Diaspora). These Jewish Christians, like many other believers of the day, were enduring persecution at the hands of non-believers and also experiencing extreme financial hardship. James seems to have in mind for his letter an audience of these poorer "dispersed" Jewish Christians but also their wealthier non-Jewish counterparts, as he challenges both the impoverished and those with resources to care for one another and draw on God's wisdom to handle their difficult situation (see 1:5–8).

KEY THEMES

- God gives us true wisdom.
- Satan tempts to break us; God tests to strengthen us.
- The words we use are powerful and influential.
- Faith and good deeds go hand in hand.

KEY VERSE

As the body without the spirit is dead, so faith without deeds is dead (James 2:26).

CONTENTS

LESSON ONE

GROWING THROUGH TRIALS

My brethren, count it all joy when you fall into various trials, knowing that the testing of your faith produces patience.
JAMES 1:2–3 NKJV

REFLECTION

The letter of James deals with the "practical" side of faith, which means trusting God even in times difficulties and crises. Think about the way you have responded to a recent problem or struggle in your life. How would you describe your general attitude during this time? What does your response to this situation reveal about your view of God?

_____

_____

_____

_____

_____

_____

_____

_____

_____

_____

_____

_____

_____

_____

_____

_____

_____

_____

_____

_____

_____

_____

SITUATION

Like many of the early church leaders, James served under the continual threat of trials and violence. Both the Roman authorities and the Jewish religious leaders had reasons to persecute as many Christians as possible. To the Romans, the Christians were troublemakers. To the Jewish leaders, they were blasphemers. James wrote to his fellow believers in part to encourage them to persevere in the midst of all these trials. He reminds them of the benefits they can expect to receive from hardships and the importance of living genuine lives of faith.

OBSERVATION

Read James 1:1–11 from the New International Version or the New King James Version.

NEW INTERNATIONAL VERSION

[1] James, a servant of God and of the Lord Jesus Christ,

To the twelve tribes scattered among the nations:

Greetings.

[2] Consider it pure joy, my brothers and sisters, whenever you face trials of many kinds, [3] because you know that the testing of your faith produces perseverance. [4] Let perseverance finish its work so that you may be mature and complete, not lacking anything. [5] If any of you lacks wisdom, you should ask God, who gives generously to all without finding fault, and it will be given to you. [6] But when you ask, you must believe and not doubt, because the one who doubts is like a wave of the sea, blown and tossed by the wind. [7] That person should not expect to receive anything from the Lord. [8] Such a person is double-minded and unstable in all they do.

[9] Believers in humble circumstances ought to take pride in their high position. [10] But the rich should take pride in their humiliation—since they will pass away like a wild flower. [11] For the sun rises with

scorching heat and withers the plant; its blossom falls and its beauty is destroyed. In the same way, the rich will fade away even while they go about their business.

New King James Version

¹ James, a bondservant of God and of the Lord Jesus Christ,

To the twelve tribes which are scattered abroad:

Greetings.

² My brethren, count it all joy when you fall into various trials, ³ knowing that the testing of your faith produces patience. ⁴ But let patience have its perfect work, that you may be perfect and complete, lacking nothing. ⁵ If any of you lacks wisdom, let him ask of God, who gives to all liberally and without reproach, and it will be given to him. ⁶ But let him ask in faith, with no doubting, for he who doubts is like a wave of the sea driven and tossed by the wind. ⁷ For let not that man suppose that he will receive anything from the Lord; ⁸ he is a double-minded man, unstable in all his ways.

⁹ Let the lowly brother glory in his exaltation, ¹⁰ but the rich in his humiliation, because as a flower of the field he will pass away. ¹¹ For no sooner has the sun risen with a burning heat than it withers the grass; its flower falls, and its beautiful appearance perishes. So the rich man also will fade away in his pursuits.

EXPLORATION

1. How does James encourage his readers to respond to trials?

_____

_____

_____

_____

_____

_____

2. What does James mean when he says "the testing of your faith produces perseverance" (verse 3)?

_____

_____

_____

_____

_____

_____

_____

_____

3. How can you gain wisdom to deal with problems?

_____

_____

_____

_____

_____

_____

_____

_____

4. Why does God want his followers to ask for his help without doubting?

_____

_____

_____

_____

_____

_____

_____

_____

5. Who does James say should not expect to receive anything from God? Why?

_____

_____

_____

_____

_____

_____

6. Why does James say those in humble circumstances can be proud of their situation?

_____

_____

_____

_____

_____

INSPIRATION

When a potter bakes a pot, he checks its solidity by pulling it out of the oven and thumping it. If it "sings," it's ready. If it "thuds," it's placed back in the oven.

The character of a person is also checked by thumping.

Been thumped lately?

Late-night phone calls. Grouchy teacher. Grumpy moms. Burnt meals. Flat tires. You've-got-to-be-kidding deadlines. Those are thumps. Thumps are those irritating inconveniences that trigger the worst in us.

They catch us off guard. Flatfooted. They aren't big enough to be crises, but if you get enough of them, watch out! Traffic jams. Long lines. Empty mailboxes. Dirty clothes on the floor . . . *Thump. Thump. Thump.*

How do you respond? Do you sing? Or do you thud?

Jesus said that out of the nature of the heart a man speaks (see Luke 6:45). There's nothing like a good thump to reveal the nature of a heart. The true character of a person is seen not in momentary heroics, but in the thump-packed humdrum of day-to-day living. . . .

Have you felt the divine Potter's thump lately? Why do you think he might be testing you? And if it's been a while since you've been thumped, why do you think that is? (From *Shaped by God* by Max Lucado.)

REACTION

7. How have some recent "thumps" challenged you to seek God?

_____

_____

_____

_____

_____

_____

_____

8. How do you usually respond to life's difficulties?

_____

_____

_____

_____

_____

_____

9. How has your relationship with God changed as you have gone through trials?

_____

_____

_____

_____

_____

_____

_____

10. Why is it so hard to respond with joy when you are faced with problems?

_____

_____

_____

_____

_____

_____

_____

_____

11. How have you seen God bring good into your life through trials?

_____

_____

_____

_____

_____

_____

_____

12. When was a time that God's wisdom helped you get through a problem?

_____

_____

_____

_____

_____

_____

_____

_____

_____

_____

LIFE LESSONS

Many of us have a contingency plan for _if_ things go wrong. In truth, we need a plan for _when_ things go bad. If we assume life is trouble-free, we will have to deal with constant disappointment. But if we realize life involves a mixture of troubles and blessings, we will have better reason to plan with hardships in mind. Trouble may not be here in the moment, but it's coming. James helps us to see that God even allows trouble for our good. He doesn't want us to worry about _why_ troubles come. He wants us to prepare and trust him _when_ troubles come.

DEVOTION

Father, we come to you just as we are, struggling to cope with the trials of life. We are grateful that you never turn your back on us. You promise to give us the wisdom and strength we need to face each day. Continue to test us until our character shines and brings glory to you.

JOURNALING

How can you grow closer to God through the trials you are facing right now?

_____

_____

_____

_____

_____

_____

_____

_____

_____

_____

_____

_____

_____

_____

_____

_____

_____

_____

_____

FOR FURTHER READING

To complete the book of James during this twelve-part study, read James 1:1–11. For more Bible passages on growing through trials, see Romans 5:3–5; 2 Corinthians 4:16–18; 6:3–10; 2 Thessalonians 1:3–4; and 1 Peter 1:5–7; 4:12–14.

ENDURING TEMPTATION

Blessed is the one who perseveres under trial because, having stood the test, that person will receive the crown of life that the Lord has promised to those who love him.

JAMES 1:12

REFLECTION

One of the classic hymns of the church is "Count Your Blessings." The song highlights the fact that we often tend to tally our temptations, trials, and complaints rather than our blessings. Take two minutes right now to compile a short list of all the items and people you consider to be God's blessings in your life. In what ways have you received good gifts from God?

SITUATION

James has encouraged his readers to actually take *joy* in the many trials they are facing, pointing them to the fact that such struggles leads to the development of perseverance and faith in their lives. He now moves on to another source of encouragement: God's good gifts and blessings. James understands that his readers—ourselves included—will face temptations of all kinds. Our own evil desires will tempt us to sin. But as followers of Jesus, we have plenty of reasons for joyful living, for we can know that God is consistently working for our good.

OBSERVATION

Read James 1:12–18 from the New International Version or the New King James Version.

New International Version

[12] Blessed is the one who perseveres under trial because, having stood the test, that person will receive the crown of life that the Lord has promised to those who love him.

[13] When tempted, no one should say, "God is tempting me." For God cannot be tempted by evil, nor does he tempt anyone; [14] but each person is tempted when they are dragged away by their own evil desire and enticed. [15] Then, after desire has conceived, it gives birth to sin; and sin, when it is full-grown, gives birth to death.

[16] Don't be deceived, my dear brothers and sisters. [17] Every good and perfect gift is from above, coming down from the Father of the heavenly lights, who does not change like shifting shadows. [18] He chose to give us birth through the word of truth, that we might be a kind of firstfruits of all he created.

New King James Version

[12] Blessed is the man who endures temptation; for when he has been approved, he will receive the crown of life which the Lord has promised to

those who love Him. [13] Let no one say when he is tempted, "I am tempted by God"; for God cannot be tempted by evil, nor does He Himself tempt anyone. [14] But each one is tempted when he is drawn away by his own desires and enticed. [15] Then, when desire has conceived, it gives birth to sin; and sin, when it is full-grown, brings forth death.

[16] Do not be deceived, my beloved brethren. [17] Every good gift and every perfect gift is from above, and comes down from the Father of lights, with whom there is no variation or shadow of turning. [18] Of His own will He brought us forth by the word of truth, that we might be a kind of firstfruits of His creatures.

EXPLORATION

1. Why does James say the person who endures under trials is blessed?

_____

_____

_____

_____

_____

_____

_____

2. How does God reward those who are faithful to him?

_____

_____

_____

_____

_____

_____

3. Why is it easy to blame God as the source of temptation?

4. How does James explain the true source of temptations?

5. What are the results of continually giving in to sin?

6. How does James say that God rescued you from evil desires?

_____

_____

_____

_____

_____

_____

_____

_____

_____

INSPIRATION

Victor Hugo introduced us a character known as Jean Valjean in the classic _Les Misérables_. Valjean enters the pages as a vagabond. A just-released prisoner in midlife, wearing threadbare trousers and a tattered jacket. Nineteen years in a French prison have left him rough and fearless. He's walked for four days in the Alpine chill of nineteenth-century southeastern France, only to find that no inn will take him, no tavern will feed him. Finally he knocks on the door of a bishop's house.

Monseigneur Myriel is seventy-five years old. Like Valjean, he has lost much. The revolution took all the valuables from his family except some silverware, a soup ladle, and two candlesticks. Valjean tells his story and expects the religious man to turn him away. But the bishop is kind. He asks the visitor to sit near a fire. "You did not need to tell me who you were," he explains. "This is not my house—it is the house of Jesus Christ." After some time the bishop takes the ex-convict to the table, where they dine on soup and bread, figs, and cheese with wine, using the bishop's fine silverware.

He shows Valjean to a bedroom. In spite of the comfort, the ex-prisoner can't sleep. In spite of the kindness of the bishop, he can't resist the temptation. He stuffs the silverware into his knapsack. The priest sleeps through the robbery, and Valjean runs into the night.

But he doesn't get far. The policemen catch him and march him back to the bishop's house. Valjean knows what his capture means—prison for the rest of his life. But then something wonderful happens. Before the officer can explain the crime, the bishop steps forward.

"Oh! Here you are! I'm so glad to see you. I can't believe you forgot the candlesticks! They are made of pure silver as well . . . please take them with the forks and spoons I gave you."

Valjean is stunned. The bishop dismisses the policemen and then turns and says, "Jean Valjean, my brother, you no longer belong to evil, but to good. I have bought your soul from you. I take it back from evil thoughts and deeds and the Spirit of Hell, and I give it to God."

Valjean has a choice: believe the priest or believe his past. Jean Valjean believes the priest. He becomes the mayor of a small town. He builds a factory and gives jobs to the poor. He takes pity on a dying mother and raises her daughter.

Grace changed him. Let it change you. (From *Grace* by Max Lucado.)

REACTION

7. In what ways is God like the merciful bishop in this story?

_____

_____

_____

_____

_____

_____

_____

_____

_____

8. Is temptation itself *sin*? How are the two related?

_____

_____

_____

_____

_____

_____

_____

9. How has God's grace changed you when you have fallen prey to temptation?

_____

_____

_____

_____

_____

_____

_____

10. How does knowing God is good encourage you to fight against sin in your life?

_____

_____

_____

_____

_____

_____

_____

11. How has the testimony of other believers helped you in your struggle against sin?

12. What are some ways you can depend more on God for the strength to overcome sin?

LIFE LESSONS

We can do two things when we encounter temptation: run from it or face it. Both actions are forms of resistance. The ones we must face with God's wisdom are often the *internal* ones—the ones from which we can't very well run away. These are temptations such as fear, selfishness, pride, and the like . . . which we must resist with the truth of God's Word. The temptations we should avoid or flee are the *external* ones—much as Joseph did when he ran away from the advances of Potiphar's seductive wife. In *every* temptation we need God's help. We need to ask God what we can learn from a temptation we face instead of relying on our own human wisdom and questioning God's motives.

DEVOTION

Father, when we confront temptation—whether internal or external—we pray that you would give us the strength to resist it. Thank you for your promise that if we do what is right, we can know that eventually truth, justice, and goodness will prevail.

JOURNALING

How has God set you free from sin and temptation?

FOR FURTHER READING

To complete the book of James during this twelve-part study, read James 1:12–18. For more Bible passages on temptation, read Matthew 6:13; 26:41; Luke 4:1–2; Romans 8:5–8; 1 Corinthians 10:13; Galatians 6:1; Ephesians 6:11–13; and Hebrews 4:15–16.

LESSON THREE

LISTENING AND DOING

He who looks into the perfect law of liberty and continues in it, and is not a forgetful hearer but a doer of the work, this one will be blessed in what he does.

JAMES 1:25 NKJV

REFLECTION

Godliness is not a trait that any of us would likely list on a résumé. The word is difficult to clearly define—and yet in our extended relationships with other believers, we can usually tell who has made progress in godliness. Think of one person in your circle of relationships who truly exemplifies godliness. How has that person's life been an example to you?

_____

_____

_____

_____

_____

_____

_____

_____

_____

_____

_____

_____

_____

_____

_____

_____

_____

_____

_____

SITUATION

James continues his teaching by challenging his readers in the practical areas of *listening* and *doing*. He begins by noting that sometimes we need to just be quiet and listen to other people, while at other times we need to get busy in doing what God's Word has instructed us to do—particularly as it relates to loving one another. As James shows, we can tell we are listening *constructively* when God's Word begins to change how we see ourselves and how we see other people. True godliness will then be seen in our being and doing.

OBSERVATION

Read James 1:19–27 from the New International Version or the New King James Version.

New International Version

¹⁹ My dear brothers and sisters, take note of this. Everyone should be quick to listen, slow to speak and slow to become angry, ²⁰ because human anger does not produce the righteousness that God desires. ²¹ Therefore, get rid of all moral filth and the evil that is so prevalent and humbly accept the word planted in you, which can save you.

²² Do not merely listen to the word, and so deceive yourselves. Do what it says. ²³ Anyone who listens to the word but does not do what it says is like someone who looks at his face in a mirror ²⁴ and, after looking at himself, goes away and immediately forgets what he looks like. ²⁵ But whoever looks intently into the perfect law that gives freedom, and continues in it—not forgetting what they have heard, but doing it—they will be blessed in what they do.

²⁶ Those who consider themselves religious and yet do not keep a tight rein on their tongues deceive themselves, and their religion is worthless. ²⁷ Religion that God our Father accepts as pure and faultless is this: to look after orphans and widows in their distress and to keep oneself from being polluted by the world.

New King James Version

¹⁹ So then, my beloved brethren, let every man be swift to hear, slow to speak, slow to wrath; ²⁰ for the wrath of man does not produce the right-eousness of God.

²¹ Therefore lay aside all filthiness and overflow of wickedness, and receive with meekness the implanted word, which is able to save your souls.

²² But be doers of the word, and not hearers only, deceiving your-selves. ²³ For if anyone is a hearer of the word and not a doer, he is like a man observing his natural face in a mirror; ²⁴ for he observes himself, goes away, and immediately forgets what kind of man he was. ²⁵ But he who looks into the perfect law of liberty and continues in it, and is not a forgetful hearer but a doer of the work, this one will be blessed in what he does.

²⁶ If anyone among you thinks he is religious, and does not bri-dle his tongue but deceives his own heart, this one's religion is useless. ²⁷ Pure and undefiled religion before God and the Father is this: to visit orphans and widows in their trouble, and to keep oneself unspotted from the world.

EXPLORATION

1. What three steps does James encourage you to take when interacting with others?

---

2. According to James, what is the problem with human anger?

3. What are some of the ways people can deceive themselves?

4. How does James describe those who do not obey God's Word?

5. How does God bless those who study his Word and obey its teaching?

_____

_____

_____

_____

_____

_____

_____

6. How can you practice a religion that is "pure and faultless" (verse 27)?

_____

_____

_____

_____

_____

_____

_____

INSPIRATION

I'd like to tell you a story you've heard before, though you've not heard it as I am going to tell it. But you have heard it. Surely you have, for you are in it. You are one of the characters. It is the story of the dancers who had no music.

Can you imagine how hard that would be? Dancing with no music? Day after day they came to the great hall just off the corner of Main and Broadway. They brought their wives. They brought their husbands. They brought their children and their hopes. They came to dance.

The hall was prepared for a dance. Streamers strung, punch bowls filled. Chairs were placed against the walls. People arrived and sat, knowing they had come to a dance but not knowing how to dance because they had no music. They had balloons; they had cake. They even had a stage on which the musicians could play, but they had no musicians.

One time a lanky fellow claimed to be a musician. He sure looked the part, what with his belly-length beard and fancy violin. He stood before them and pulled the violin out of the case and placed it beneath his chin. *Now we will dance,* they thought, but they were wrong. For though he had a violin, his violin had no strings. The pushing and pulling of his bow sounded like the creaking of an unoiled door. Who can dance to a sound like that? . . .

Some tried to dance without the music. One wife convinced her husband to give it a try, so out on the floor they stepped, she dancing her way and he dancing his. . . . A few tried to follow their cue, but since there was no cue, they didn't know how to follow. The result was a dozen or so dancers with no music, going this way and that, bumping into each other and causing more than one observer to seek safety behind a chair.

Over time, however, those dancers grew weary, and everyone resumed the task of sitting and staring and wondering if anything was ever going to happen. And then one day it did.

Not everyone saw him enter. Only a few. Nothing about his appearance would compel your attention. His looks were common, but his music was not. He began to sing a song, soft and sweet, kind and compelling. His song took the chill out of the air and brought a summer-sunset glow to the heart.

And as he sang, people stood—a few at first, then many—and they began to dance. Together. Flowing to a music they had never heard before, they danced.

Some, however, remained seated. What kind of musician is this who never mounts the stage? Who brings no band? Who has no costume? Why, musicians don't just walk in off the street. They have an entourage, a reputation, a persona to project and protect. Why, this fellow scarcely mentioned his name!

"How can we know what you sing is actually music?" they challenged.

His reply was to the point: "Let the man who has ears to hear use them."

But the nondancers refused to hear. So they refused to dance. Many still refuse. The musician comes and sings. Some dance. Some don't. Some find music for life; others live in silence. To those who miss the music, the musician gives the same appeal: "Let the man who has ears to hear use them." (From *Just Like Jesus* by Max Lucado.)

REACTION

7. How has your life changed since you "heard the music" and decided to follow Christ?

_____

_____

_____

_____

_____

_____

8. How can you have "ears to hear" God's Word this week . . . and then do it?

_____

_____

_____

_____

_____

9. What pressures does culture put on you to disobey or disregard God's Word?

10. What are some practical ways to protect yourself from the world's influence?

11. Why is it often so difficult to "listen to the Word" and do what you know is right?

12. In what ways do your actions demonstrate that you are a follower of Christ?

_____

_____

_____

_____

_____

_____

_____

_____

_____

_____

_____

_____

_____

LIFE LESSONS

The good news of the gospel of Christ affects the whole person. It's not a set of rules that we outwardly follow but a change deep within us that leads to a difference in our behavior. The effects of the gospel in our lives can be seen by a continual process of _inward_ transformation and then _outward_ action that honors God. God's Word frees us to live in the truth, and his Spirit gives us the power to live it out.

DEVOTION

Father, help us to hear your voice in the midst of many competing voices in the world. Help us to put into practice the timeless truths found in your Word. Most of all, help us remember that you have set us free from the lures of this world. Thank you for your promise that when the Son sets us free, we are free indeed.

JOURNALING

What are some specific ways that God has helped you to hear his Word *and* obey it?

_____

_____

_____

_____

_____

_____

_____

_____

_____

_____

_____

_____

_____

_____

_____

_____

_____

_____

_____

_____

_____

_____

_____

_____

_____

FOR FURTHER READING

To complete the book of James during this twelve-part study, read James 1:19–27. For more Bible passages on obedience, read Deuteronomy 28:1–14; Isaiah 1:18–20; Acts 5:27–32; Romans 6:1–14; Titus 3:1–2; Hebrews 12:13–14; 1 Peter 1:13–15; 1 John 3:24; and 2 John 1:6.

LESSON FOUR

EQUALITY IN THE CHURCH

If you really keep the royal law found in Scripture, "Love your neighbor as yourself," you are doing right. But if you show favoritism, you sin and are convicted by the law as lawbreakers.

JAMES 2:8–9

REFLECTION

Look around and you'll see that it's human nature to revere the wealthy and look down on the poor. Part of being doers of the Word is going against "nature" and not treating people with favoritism, especially in the church. Reflect on a time when you attended a church as a visitor, and think about the positive and negative parts of that experience. When people visit your church, how do you make them feel welcome?

SITUATION

In this next section of his letter, James turns his attention toward some of the more practical issues that are occurring among believers in the early church, including the matter of favoritism and judging others fairly. In the atmosphere that existed in the early church, it appears many believers were tempted to treat any prestigious visitors with special deference and grant privileges to the wealthy not extended to other guests. James is determined to confront this partiality that threatens to undermine the gospel and socially fragment the church by prescribing what he knows to be the antidote for the problem: God's royal law of love.

OBSERVATION

Read James 2:1–13 from the New International
Version or the New King James Version.

NEW INTERNATIONAL VERSION

[1] My brothers and sisters, believers in our glorious Lord Jesus Christ must not show favoritism. [2] Suppose a man comes into your meeting wearing a gold ring and fine clothes, and a poor man in filthy old clothes also comes in. [3] If you show special attention to the man wearing fine clothes and say, "Here's a good seat for you," but say to the poor man, "You stand there" or "Sit on the floor by my feet," [4] have you not discriminated among yourselves and become judges with evil thoughts?

[5] Listen, my dear brothers and sisters: Has not God chosen those who are poor in the eyes of the world to be rich in faith and to inherit the kingdom he promised those who love him? [6] But you have dishonored the poor. Is it not the rich who are exploiting you? Are they not the ones who are dragging you into court? [7] Are they not the ones who are blaspheming the noble name of him to whom you belong?

[8] If you really keep the royal law found in Scripture, "Love your neighbor as yourself," you are doing right. [9] But if you show favoritism,

you sin and are convicted by the law as lawbreakers. [10] For whoever keeps the whole law and yet stumbles at just one point is guilty of breaking all of it. [11] For he who said, "You shall not commit adultery," also said, "You shall not murder." If you do not commit adultery but do commit murder, you have become a lawbreaker.

[12] Speak and act as those who are going to be judged by the law that gives freedom, [13] because judgment without mercy will be shown to anyone who has not been merciful. Mercy triumphs over judgment.

New King James Version

[1] My brethren, do not hold the faith of our Lord Jesus Christ, the Lord of glory, with partiality. [2] For if there should come into your assembly a man with gold rings, in fine apparel, and there should also come in a poor man in filthy clothes, [3] and you pay attention to the one wearing the fine clothes and say to him, "You sit here in a good place," and say to the poor man, "You stand there," or, "Sit here at my footstool," [4] have you not shown partiality among yourselves, and become judges with evil thoughts?

[5] Listen, my beloved brethren: Has God not chosen the poor of this world to be rich in faith and heirs of the kingdom which He promised to those who love Him? [6] But you have dishonored the poor man. Do not the rich oppress you and drag you into the courts? [7] Do they not blaspheme that noble name by which you are called?

[8] If you really fulfill the royal law according to the Scripture, "You shall love your neighbor as yourself," you do well; [9] but if you show partiality, you commit sin, and are convicted by the law as transgressors. [10] For whoever shall keep the whole law, and yet stumble in one point, he is guilty of all. [11] For He who said, "Do not commit adultery," also said, "Do not murder." Now if you do not commit adultery, but you do murder, you have become a transgressor of the law. [12] So speak and so do as those who will be judged by the law of liberty. [13] For judgment is without mercy to the one who has shown no mercy. Mercy triumphs over judgment.

EXPLORATION

1. What situation was occurring in the congregations that James was addressing?

_____

_____

_____

_____

_____

_____

2. Why does James say it wrong to consider some in the church as being better than others?

_____

_____

_____

_____

_____

_____

3. How does James say that partiality makes a person an "unjust judge"?

_____

_____

_____

_____

_____

_____

4. How does showing favoritism indicate you are not keeping the royal law found in Scripture to "love your neighbor as yourself" (verse 8)?

_____

_____

_____

_____

_____

5. How does _God_ treat the poor and powerless?

_____

_____

_____

_____

6. What are some of the ways a believer in Christ can show mercy to others?

_____

_____

_____

_____

_____

INSPIRATION

The church often resembles a family on summer vacation. You know the experience. You pile in the car and hit the road. Initially, the enthusiasm soars and moods are good. But 300 miles of interstate eventually takes a toll. Johnny uses too much of the seat. Heather won't share her pillow. Dad refuses to ask for directions. Mom has to stop at the restroom again.

Candy and car snacks fall on the carpet. Feet smell, and tension swells. There is a time in every trip when each family member has this thought: *I'm getting out of the car. I'll hitchhike. I'll walk. I'll do anything. Just get me out of this car.*

But do we? No, we stay in the car. Why? Well, one, we can't reach the destination alone, and two, we are family.

Can't the same be said about Christians in a congregation? We don't spill the candy, but we spill the beans. Our feet may not stink, but our attitudes do. We grow weary of one another. Some start to smell. But do we get out of the car?

No. Why? Because we know that apart from the Father, we can't reach the destination. And, besides, we are family.

Not always easy, is it? I once saw a person on a religious broadcast with poofy hair and pink clothes and bright shoes, and you should have seen how his wife was dressed. How can we be in the same family? I wondered. The answer came as they began to speak. They spoke genuinely of Christ on the cross. They spoke of grace for all sin. I'm not too keen on the way they look, but I love the One to whom they look. And since we look to the same One, are we not family?

Then there is the fellow with whom I disagree about everything. Politics. Ethics. What he sees as important doctrine, I see as tradition. What I see as necessary change, he sees as rocking the boat. I've never known a man with such poor judgment. But each Sunday we sit in the same church. Each Sunday we partake of the same bread and drink of the same cup. And each Sunday I'm reminded: the Lord determines who sits at the table, not me. And if the Lord invites him and me to the same table, are we not family?

We dress differently. We think differently. We are different. But if we're in the same car, being driven by the same Father, headed toward the same place, can we not accept one another? (From *Max on Life* by Max Lucado.)

REACTION

7. In what ways is your church like "a family on summer vacation"?

8. What are some of the causes of tension in your church?

9. What are some general examples of favoritism or prejudice you see in the church today?

10. How does remembering that you and other believers are all part of the same family—and all serve the same Lord—help you to deal with favoritism or prejudice?

11. Who are some people in your world who might feel uncomfortable in your church?

_____

_____

_____

_____

_____

_____

_____

12. What would happen if Jesus brought some of those people to your church next week?

_____

_____

_____

_____

_____

_____

LIFE LESSONS

James's words in this passage allow no wiggle room for ambiguity—"if you show favoritism, you sin and are convicted by the law as lawbreakers" (2:9). Favoritism is based on prejudice and judging others by false standards. It flourishes when we stop looking at people the way God looks at them—and this also means we have stopped seeing _ourselves_ as God sees us. We need to ask God to help us identify our prejudices and recognize situations in which we tend to show favoritism. We need to actively resist these tendencies, asking others to keep us accountable.

DEVOTION

Thank you, Father, that all people are equal in your eyes. Forgive us for judging people by appearances and accomplishments. Forgive us for favoring the rich and powerful over the poor and weak. Lord, change our hearts. Teach us what it means to love our neighbors as ourselves.

JOURNALING

How can you really keep the "royal law" found in Scripture and not show favoritism to others?

_____

_____

_____

_____

_____

_____

_____

_____

_____

_____

_____

_____

_____

_____

_____

_____

_____

_____

FOR FURTHER READING

To complete the book of James during this twelve-part study, read James 2:1–13. For more Bible passages on favoritism, read Exodus 23:1–3; Leviticus 19:15; Deuteronomy 10:14–19; Mark 12:30–31; Acts 10:34–43; Romans 2:6–11; Ephesians 6:9; and 1 Timothy 5:17–21.

LESSON FIVE

HOW FAITH WORKS

*As the body without the spirit is dead,
so faith without works is dead also.*
JAMES 2:26 NKJV

REFLECTION

When several people pool their efforts and resources together to meet a crisis, an amazing dynamic seems to take place. Perhaps the benefits of working together are almost as great as the benefits of helping someone. Think of a time when you saw a group of people rally around someone in need. What motivated the group to help that person? What was the result?

_____

_____

_____

_____

_____

_____

_____

_____

_____

_____

_____

_____

_____

SITUATION

As previously noted, James is writing to believers who have been "scattered among the nations" (James 1:1). Given this, he addresses broader issues of faith that are not locked in to a particular culture, location, or situation. One of these issues that James will now explore is the relationship between a Christ-follower's *beliefs* and how those beliefs should shape his or her *actions*. In his blunt manner, James minces no words when it comes to expressing his view that "faith without deeds is useless" (2:20). He also draws on some heavy-duty Old Testament examples to support his argument that a believer's life should be *active* and *proactive*.

OBSERVATION

Read James 2:14–26 from the New International Version or the New King James Version.

NEW INTERNATIONAL VERSION

14 What good is it, my brothers and sisters, if someone claims to have faith but has no deeds? Can such faith save them? 15 Suppose a brother or a sister is without clothes and daily food. 16 If one of you says to them, "Go in peace; keep warm and well fed," but does nothing about their physical needs, what good is it? 17 In the same way, faith by itself, if it is not accompanied by action, is dead.

18 But someone will say, "You have faith; I have deeds."

Show me your faith without deeds, and I will show you my faith by my deeds. 19 You believe that there is one God. Good! Even the demons believe that—and shudder.

20 You foolish person, do you want evidence that faith without deeds is useless? 21 Was not our father Abraham considered righteous for what he did when he offered his son Isaac on the altar? 22 You see that his faith and his actions were working together, and his faith was made complete by what he did. 23 And the scripture was fulfilled that says, "Abraham believed God, and it was credited to him as righteousness," and he was called God's friend. 24 You see that a person is considered righteous by what they do and not by faith alone.

25 In the same way, was not even Rahab the prostitute considered righteous for what she did when she gave lodging to the spies and sent them off in a different direction? 26 As the body without the spirit is dead, so faith without deeds is dead.

New King James Version

¹⁴ What does it profit, my brethren, if someone says he has faith but does not have works? Can faith save him? ¹⁵ If a brother or sister is naked and destitute of daily food, ¹⁶ and one of you says to them, "Depart in peace, be warmed and filled," but you do not give them the things which are needed for the body, what does it profit? ¹⁷ Thus also faith by itself, if it does not have works, is dead.

¹⁸ But someone will say, "You have faith, and I have works." Show me your faith without your works, and I will show you my faith by my works. ¹⁹ You believe that there is one God. You do well. Even the demons believe—and tremble! ²⁰ But do you want to know, O foolish man, that faith without works is dead? ²¹ Was not Abraham our father justified by works when he offered Isaac his son on the altar? ²² Do you see that faith was working together with his works, and by works faith was made perfect? ²³ And the Scripture was fulfilled which says, "Abraham believed God, and it was accounted to him for righteousness." And he was called the friend of God. ²⁴ You see then that a man is justified by works, and not by faith only.

²⁵ Likewise, was not Rahab the harlot also justified by works when she received the messengers and sent them out another way?

²⁶ For as the body without the spirit is dead, so faith without works is dead also.

EXPLORATION

1. Why is faith "dead" if it is not accompanied by works?

_____

_____

_____

_____

_____

2. How do believers demonstrate their living faith in Christ?

3. How do some people rationalize inactive faith?

4. Why is not enough to merely *believe* there is one God?

5. Read Genesis 22:1–12. How did Abraham demonstrate his faith in this story?

_____

_____

_____

_____

_____

_____

_____

6. Read Joshua 2:1–14. How did Rahab demonstrate her faith in this story?

_____

_____

_____

_____

_____

_____

_____

INSPIRATION

You and I have the privilege to do for others what God does for us. How do we show people that we believe in them? *Show up.* Nothing takes the place of your presence. Letters are nice. Phone calls are special. But being there in the flesh sends a message . . .

Do you believe in your kids? Then show up. Show up at their games. Show up at their plays. Show up at their recitals. It may not be possible to make each one, but it's sure worth the effort. An elder in our church supports me with his presence. Whenever I speak at an area congregation, he'll show up. Does nothing. Says little. Just takes a seat in a pew and smiles when we make eye contact. It means a lot to me. In fact, as I write this, he is one room away. Made the ninety-minute drive from his house to my hideout just to pray for me.

Do you believe in your friends? Then show up. Show up at their graduations and weddings. Spend time with them. You want to bring out the best in someone? Then show up.

Listen up. You don't have to speak to encourage. The Bible says, "It is best to listen much, speak little" (James 1:19 TLB). We tend to speak much and listen little. There is a time to speak. But there is also a time to be quiet.

That's what my father did. Dropping a fly ball may not be a big deal to most people, but if you are thirteen years old and have aspirations of the big leagues, it is a big deal. Not only was it my second error of the game, it allowed the winning run to score.

I didn't even go back to the dugout. I turned around in the middle of left field and climbed over the fence. I was halfway home when my dad found me. He didn't say a word. Just pulled over to the side of the road, leaned across the seat, and opened the passenger door. We didn't speak. We didn't need to. We both knew the world had come to an end. When we got home, I went straight to my room, and he went straight to the kitchen. Presently he appeared in front of me with cookies and milk . . . Dad never said a word. But he did show up. . . .

Speak up. Nathaniel Hawthorne came home heartbroken. He'd just been fired from his job in the custom house. His wife, rather than responding with anxiety, surprised him with joy. "Now you can write your book!"

He wasn't so positive. "And what shall we live on while I'm writing it?"

To his amazement she opened a drawer and revealed a wad of currency she'd saved out of her housekeeping budget. "I always knew you were a man of genius," she told him. "I always knew you'd write a masterpiece."

She believed in her husband. And because she did, he wrote. And because he wrote, every library in America has a copy of *The Scarlet Letter* by Nathaniel Hawthorne.

You also have the power to change someone's life simply by the words that you speak. "The tongue has the power of life and death" (Proverbs 18:21). (From *A Love Worth Giving* by Max Lucado.)

REACTION

7. What are some ways to "show up" and practice your faith through your words and actions?

_____

_____

_____

_____

8. What are some ways you can better "listen up" to show you support another person?

_____

_____

_____

9. What are some situations in which you need to "speak up" to encourage a friend?

_____

_____

_____

10. Why do you think the Bible stresses the importance of helping others?

_____

_____

_____

_____

_____

11. How is helping others part of a disciplined spiritual life?

_____

_____

_____

_____

_____

12. Who specifically will you reach out to help today to show your faith in action?

_____

_____

_____

_____

LIFE LESSONS

The Bible describes faith as belief that results in a dynamic and active response to God's grace. The _belief_ part focuses on trust in God, while the _active_ part focuses on gratitude for what he has done and obedience to his Word. Faith is not "belief in works" or even "belief in faith" but works coming out of a settled trust in God. Both workless faith and faithless work fall short. Authentic faith trusts _and_ obeys.

DEVOTION

Father, thank you for your perfect plan of salvation. Thank you for providing a way for us to spend eternity with you. Until then, help us to demonstrate our faith not only through our words but also through our actions. Show us the good work you want us to do and give us the strength to do it.

JOURNALING

How do faith and works go together in your life?

_____

_____

_____

_____

_____

_____

_____

_____

_____

_____

_____

_____

_____

_____

_____

_____

FOR FURTHER READING

To complete the book of James during this twelve-part study, read James 2:14–26. For more Bible passages on faith and works, read Matthew 5:14–16; John 14:9–12; Ephesians 2:8–10; Philippians 2:14–17; 2 Thessalonians 1:11–12; Hebrews 6:9–12; and 2 Peter 1:5–7.

TAMING THE TONGUE

*Out of the same mouth proceed
blessing and cursing. My brethren,
these things ought not to be so.*
JAMES 3:10 NKJV

REFLECTION

A pinch of salt in a wound, a pebble in a shoe, and a nail in a tire are all small items that can result in great consequences. Think of some other examples of this principle. What are some tiny objects that wield great power or influence? Why are these things easy to overlook?

_____

_____

_____

_____

_____

_____

_____

_____

_____

_____

_____

_____

_____

_____

_____

_____

SITUATION

For James, it was not enough for people to just *say* they had faith. People also needed to demonstrate that faith through their *actions*. While James understood it was faith in Christ that saved a person, he firmly believed the outflow of that faith would naturally result in observable actions of love and service toward one another. He wasn't impressed by empty words . . . and yet he certainly appreciated the awesome power contained in human speech. In this next section of his letter, he focuses on a small part of the human body that we often overlook—the tongue—and shows how it can be used for great good or great evil.

OBSERVATION

Read James 3:1–12 from the New International Version or the New King James Version.

NEW INTERNATIONAL VERSION

[1] Not many of you should become teachers, my fellow believers, because you know that we who teach will be judged more strictly. [2] We all stumble in many ways. Anyone who is never at fault in what they say is perfect, able to keep their whole body in check.

[3] When we put bits into the mouths of horses to make them obey us, we can turn the whole animal. [4] Or take ships as an example. Although they are so large and are driven by strong winds, they are steered by a very small rudder wherever the pilot wants to go. [5] Likewise, the tongue is a small part of the body, but it makes great boasts. Consider what a great forest is set on fire by a small spark. [6] The tongue also is a fire, a world of evil among the parts of the body. It corrupts the whole body, sets the whole course of one's life on fire, and is itself set on fire by hell.

[7] All kinds of animals, birds, reptiles and sea creatures are being tamed and have been tamed by mankind, [8] but no human being can tame the tongue. It is a restless evil, full of deadly poison.

[9] With the tongue we praise our Lord and Father, and with it we curse human beings, who have been made in God's likeness. [10] Out of the same mouth come praise and cursing. My brothers and sisters, this should not be. [11] Can both fresh water and salt water flow from the same spring? [12] My brothers and sisters, can a fig tree bear olives, or a grape-vine bear figs? Neither can a salt spring produce fresh water.

New King James Version

¹ My brethren, let not many of you become teachers, knowing that we shall receive a stricter judgment. ² For we all stumble in many things. If anyone does not stumble in word, he is a perfect man, able also to bridle the whole body. ³ Indeed, we put bits in horses' mouths that they may obey us, and we turn their whole body. ⁴ Look also at ships: although they are so large and are driven by fierce winds, they are turned by a very small rudder wherever the pilot desires. ⁵ Even so the tongue is a little member and boasts great things.

See how great a forest a little fire kindles! ⁶ And the tongue is a fire, a world of iniquity. The tongue is so set among our members that it defiles the whole body, and sets on fire the course of nature; and it is set on fire by hell. ⁷ For every kind of beast and bird, of reptile and creature of the sea, is tamed and has been tamed by mankind. ⁸ But no man can tame the tongue. It is an unruly evil, full of deadly poison. ⁹ With it we bless our God and Father, and with it we curse men, who have been made in the similitude of God. ¹⁰ Out of the same mouth proceed blessing and cursing. My brethren, these things ought not to be so. ¹¹ Does a spring send forth fresh water and bitter from the same opening? ¹² Can a fig tree, my brethren, bear olives, or a grapevine bear figs? Thus no spring yields both salt water and fresh.

EXPLORATION

1. Why does James give such a stern warning in this passage to those who want to be teachers?

_____

_____

_____

_____

_____

_____

2. How does a person's tongue (or speech) compare to a horse's bit and a ship's rudder?

_____

_____

_____

_____

_____

_____

_____

_____

3. In what ways is the tongue like fire?

_____

_____

_____

_____

_____

_____

_____

_____

4. Why is the tongue so difficult to "tame" or control?

_____

_____

_____

_____

_____

_____

_____

_____

5. How can the tongue can be used for both good and evil?

_____

_____

_____

_____

6. How has this passage helped you to see the power of your words?

_____

_____

_____

_____

INSPIRATION

Our words have power . . . for good or evil. And words spoken over us can also have a lot of power . . . for good or evil. So, how do we handle a situation where we find that a friend we thought we could trust is saying mean comments behind our back?

I am reminded of a person in our world who once brought my wife, Denalyn, and me a lot of stress. She would call in the middle of the night. She was demanding and ruthless. She screamed at us in public. When she wanted something, she wanted it immediately, and she wanted it exclusively from us.

But we never asked her to leave us alone. We never told her to bug someone else. We never tried to get even.

After all, she was only a few months old.

It was easy for us to forgive our infant daughter's behavior because we knew she didn't know better.

Now, there is a world of difference between an innocent child and a deliberate destroyer. But there is still a point to my story: the way to handle a person's behavior is to understand the cause of it. One way to deal with people's peculiarities is to try to understand why they are peculiar.

Jesus knew Judas had been seduced by a powerful foe. He was aware of the wiles of Satan's whispers (he had just heard them himself). He knew how hard it was for Judas to do what was right.

He didn't justify what Judas did. He didn't minimize the deed. Nor did he release Judas from his choice. But he did look eye to eye at his betrayer and try to understand.

As long as you hate your enemy, a jail door is closed, and a prisoner is taken. But when you try to understand and release your foe from your hatred, then the prisoner is released, and that prisoner is you. (From *Max on Life* by Max Lucado.)

REACTION

7. What are some situations in your life when a person's words has caused you harm?

_____

_____

_____

_____

8. How did you respond in those situations? Looking back, do you have any regrets?

_____

_____

_____

_____

9. How can understanding the cause of a person's behavior—and words toward you—help you to deal with the conflict in a healthy way?

_____

_____

_____

_____

_____

_____

10. When are some times in your life when a person's words brought you encouragement?

_____

_____

_____

_____

_____

_____

11. How are you actively seeking to encourage others through your words?

_____

_____

_____

_____

_____

12. Why is it important to submit your tongue to the control of God's Spirit every day?

_____

_____

_____

_____

_____

_____

_____

_____

_____

_____

LIFE LESSONS

In the big picture of faith and works, James says our speech is the number one indicator of what we believe. James doesn't want us to convey mixed messages. If the way we speak turns people away, our faith in action may never get a chance to touch their lives. Given this, we need to consider how others would describe the color and content of our words. Is what we are saying true? Is it necessary? Does it lift others up or tear them down? Does our speech truly honor God? We need to look at the big picture and not our immediate reactions.

DEVOTION

Father, change us from the inside out. Purify our hearts so our speech will be pleasing to you. Keep us from using our words to manipulate and hurt others. Empower us by your Holy Spirit to use our tongues to sing your praises and to build others up in the faith.

JOURNALING

What can you do to better let God control the words you say?

_____
_____
_____
_____
_____
_____
_____
_____
_____
_____
_____
_____
_____
_____
_____
_____
_____
_____
_____
_____
_____

FOR FURTHER READING

To complete the book of James during this twelve-part study, read James 3:1–12. For more Bible passages on controlling the tongue, read Leviticus 19:16–18; Psalm 34:8–14; Proverbs 12:18; 13:3; 21:23; Ephesians 4:29–32; Titus 3:1–2; and 1 Peter 3:9–12.

SOWING SEEDS OF PEACE

Now the fruit of righteousness is sown in peace by those who make peace.
JAMES 3:18 NKJV

REFLECTION

In the middle of conflict, some people use a soothing tone of voice. Some speak firmly while never raising their voices. Others wait patiently until all the verbal heat is spent before they respond. Think of a time when you saw someone bring peace to a volatile situation or light to a dark place. How did that person accomplish it?

_____

_____

_____

_____

_____

_____

_____

_____

_____

_____

_____

_____

_____

_____

_____

_____

_____

_____

_____

_____

_____

SITUATION

James has previously noted that true wisdom is a gift from God that believers in Christ can obtain when they ask for it with confidence and expectation of receiving it (see 1:5–6). In this next section of his letter, he goes on to show what a person's life will look like when he or she has truly embraced this gift from above—and what that person's life will look like if he or she has embraced another kind of "wisdom" that does not come from God. In many ways, James's words in this passage echo Jesus' statements in the Sermon on the Mount, especially where Christ says that peacemakers "will be called children of God" (Matthew 5:9).

OBSERVATION

Read James 3:13–18 from the New International
Version or the New King James Version.

NEW INTERNATIONAL VERSION

¹³ Who is wise and understanding among you? Let them show it by their good life, by deeds done in the humility that comes from wisdom. ¹⁴ But if you harbor bitter envy and selfish ambition in your hearts, do not boast about it or deny the truth. ¹⁵ Such "wisdom" does not come down from heaven but is earthly, unspiritual, demonic. ¹⁶ For where you have envy and selfish ambition, there you find disorder and every evil practice.

¹⁷ But the wisdom that comes from heaven is first of all pure; then peace-loving, considerate, submissive, full of mercy and good fruit, impartial and sincere. ¹⁸ Peacemakers who sow in peace reap a harvest of righteousness.

NEW KING JAMES VERSION

¹³ Who is wise and understanding among you? Let him show by good conduct that his works are done in the meekness of wisdom. ¹⁴ But if you have bitter envy and self-seeking in your hearts, do not boast and

lie against the truth. ¹⁵ This wisdom does not descend from above, but is earthly, sensual, demonic. ¹⁶ For where envy and self-seeking exist, confusion and every evil thing are there. ¹⁷ But the wisdom that is from above is first pure, then peaceable, gentle, willing to yield, full of mercy and good fruits, without partiality and without hypocrisy. ¹⁸ Now the fruit of righteousness is sown in peace by those who make peace.

EXPLORATION

1. How does James say people who are wise will demonstrate their wisdom?

_____

_____

_____

_____

_____

_____

2. How would you describe *worldly* wisdom?

_____

_____

_____

_____

3. How does James describe *godly* wisdom?

_____

_____

_____

_____

4. Why does envy, jealousy, and selfishness cause confusion and disorder?

_____

_____

_____

_____

_____

_____

5. What happens when people work for peace?

_____

_____

_____

_____

_____

_____

6. What are some ways you are seeking to be a peacemaker in your world?

_____

_____

_____

_____

_____

_____

INSPIRATION

As far as I know, James, the epistle writer, wasn't a farmer. But he knew the power of a seed sown in fertile soil. "Those who are peacemakers will plant seeds of peace and reap a harvest of goodness" (James 3:18 TLB).

The principle for peace is the same as the principle for crops: *never underestimate the power of a seed.*

The story of Heinz is a good example. Europe, 1934. Hitler's plague of anti-Semitism was infecting a continent. Some would escape it. Some would die from it. But eleven-year-old Heinz would learn from it. He would learn the power of sowing seeds of peace.

Heinz was a Jew.

The Bavarian village of Furth, where Heinz lived, was being overrun by Hitler's young thugs. Heinz's father, a schoolteacher, lost his job. Recreational activities ceased. Tension mounted on the streets. . . . Hitler youth roamed the neighborhoods looking for trouble. Young Heinz learned to keep his eyes open. When he saw a band of troublemakers, he would step to the other side of the street. Sometimes he would escape a fight—sometimes not.

One day, in 1934, a pivotal confrontation occurred. Heinz found himself face-to-face with a Hitler bully. A beating appeared inevitable. This time, however, he walked away unhurt—not because of what he did, but because of what he said. He didn't fight back; he spoke up. He convinced the troublemakers that a fight was not necessary. His words kept battle at bay.

And Heinz saw firsthand how the tongue can create peace.

He learned the skill of using words to avoid conflict. And for a young Jew in Hitler-ridden Europe, that skill had many opportunities to be honed.

Fortunately, Heinz's family escaped from Bavaria and made their way to America. Later in life, he would downplay the impact those adolescent experiences had on his development.

But one has to wonder. For after Heinz grew up, his name became synonymous with peace negotiations. His legacy became that of a bridge builder. Somewhere he had learned the power of the properly placed word of peace. You don't know him as Heinz. You know him by his Anglicized name, Henry. Henry Kissinger.

Never underestimate the power of a seed. (From *The Applause of Heaven* by Max Lucado.)

REACTION

7. How does a wise person resolve conflict?

_____

_____

_____

_____

8. What do you think it means to sow seeds of peace?

_____

_____

_____

_____

9. How have you seen words sown in peace produce "a harvest of righteousness" (verse 18)?

_____

_____

_____

_____

10. Why do you think people are often unwilling to work for peace?

_____

_____

_____

_____

11. How do James's words in this passage challenge you to deal with conflicts?

_____

_____

_____

_____

12. What are some practical ways you can bring peace to a conflict you are facing?

_____

_____

_____

_____

LIFE LESSONS

When we face conflict that is escalating, we need to hit the "pause" button and think it through. If envy, anger, or selfish ambition is present, wisdom is usually absent. Before we speak or engage in a conflict situation, it's wise to run our plans past the eight traits of wisdom that James listed. Is what I'm about to propose *pure, peaceable, gentle, submissive, merciful, fruitful, impartial,* and *sincere*? If our thoughts don't pass these tests, it's time to rethink.

DEVOTION

Father, thank you for the wisdom and peace you bring into our lives. Keep us from contributing to conflict instead of resolving it, and from fanning flames of discord instead of spreading peace. Give us your wisdom— wisdom to be submissive, merciful, and gentle.

JOURNALING

How can you bring a greater sense of peace to your home, work, school, and church?

FOR FURTHER READING

To complete the book of James during this twelve-part study, read James 3:13–18. For more Bible passages on wisdom and peace, read Psalms 29:11; 34:14; 119:165; Proverbs 2:6; 3:13; 4:7; Daniel 12:3; John 14:25–27; Romans 8:5–8; Philippians 4:4–7; and Colossians 2:2–3.

SUBMITTING TO GOD

Submit yourselves, then, to God. Resist the devil, and he will flee from you. Come near to God and he will come near to you.
JAMES 4:7–8

REFLECTION

According to James, we can either live for God and trust him for the outcome to any situation or live like the world and insist on claiming our rights when we feel wronged. Think of a recent conflict you had with a friend. How did you handle the dispute? What was the outcome?

_____

_____

_____

_____

_____

_____

_____

_____

_____

_____

_____

SITUATION

James has previously stated that believers will show they have truly embraced God's wisdom by the abundance of good works that are produced in their lives as a result. Having laid this framework, he can now discuss the way in which believers should apply this wisdom when it comes to handling the quarrels and conflicts that have arisen in their congregations—of which he demonstrates he is acutely aware. James especially wants his readers to understand that part of peacemaking involves a grasp on the underlying *causes* of conflicts. He lays bare the human tendency toward selfishness and insists the answer must be submission to God.

OBSERVATION

Read James 4:1–10 from the New International Version or the New King James Version.

NEW INTERNATIONAL VERSION

[1] What causes fights and quarrels among you? Don't they come from your desires that battle within you? [2] You desire but do not have, so you kill. You covet but you cannot get what you want, so you quarrel and fight. You do not have because you do not ask God. [3] When you ask, you do not receive, because you ask with wrong motives, that you may spend what you get on your pleasures.

[4] You adulterous people, don't you know that friendship with the world means enmity against God? Therefore, anyone who chooses to be a friend of the world becomes an enemy of God. [5] Or do you think Scripture says without reason that he jealously longs for the spirit he has caused to dwell in us? [6] But he gives us more grace. That is why Scripture says:

> "God opposes the proud
>> but shows favor to the humble."

[7] Submit yourselves, then, to God. Resist the devil, and he will flee from you. [8] Come near to God and he will come near to you. Wash your hands, you sinners, and purify your hearts, you double-minded. [9] Grieve, mourn and wail. Change your laughter to mourning and your joy to gloom. [10] Humble yourselves before the Lord, and he will lift you up.

NEW KING JAMES VERSION

[1] Where do wars and fights come from among you? Do they not come from your desires for pleasure that war in your members? [2] You lust and do not have. You murder and covet and cannot obtain. You fight and war. Yet you do not have because you do not ask. [3] You ask and do not

receive, because you ask amiss, that you may spend it on your pleasures. [4] Adulterers and adulteresses! Do you not know that friendship with the world is enmity with God? Whoever therefore wants to be a friend of the world makes himself an enemy of God. [5] Or do you think that the Scripture says in vain, "The Spirit who dwells in us yearns jealously"?

[6] But He gives more grace. Therefore He says:

> "God resists the proud,
> But gives grace to the humble."

[7] Therefore submit to God. Resist the devil and he will flee from you. [8] Draw near to God and He will draw near to you. Cleanse your hands, you sinners; and purify your hearts, you double-minded. [9] Lament and mourn and weep! Let your laughter be turned to mourning and your joy to gloom. [10] Humble yourselves in the sight of the Lord, and He will lift you up.

EXPLORATION

1. What causes the fights and quarrels within you and in your relationships?

_____

_____

_____

_____

2. What does James say is one reason why God may not grant a request?

_____

_____

_____

3. What does it mean to have "friendship with the world" (verse 4)?

_____

_____

_____

_____

_____

_____

4. What are some ways you can stand against the devil?

_____

_____

_____

_____

_____

5. What promise is given to those who draw near to God?

_____

_____

_____

_____

_____

_____

6. Over what does James say you are to lament and mourn?

_____

_____

_____

_____

_____

INSPIRATION

Sometime back a mother asked me to pray for her eight-year-old son. He was troubled by a constant barrage of images and scary visions. He saw people behind cars and in shadows. The images left him withdrawn and timid. They even took his sleep at night.

On the day we met he appeared defeated. His smile was gone. While his other siblings were confident and happy, there was no joy in his face. His eyes often filled with tears, and he clung to his mother.

She had taken him to doctors, but nothing had helped. Would I be willing to pray for him?

I told the young boy . . . that the devil has no authority over his life. That the real battles are fought in the mind. That God will help us take every thought captive.

I told him about the spiritual weapons of worship, Scripture, and prayer and urged him to memorize a Bible verse and quote it each time the fearful thoughts came to mind. I gave him a tool. "Reach up with your hand," I urged, "and grab the thought and throw it in the trash. And as quickly as you do that, replace it with a verse of Scripture." We then anointed him with oil and prayed.

Five days later his mother reported great progress. "Since last week the images are gone; he is no longer seeing them. He is doing well in school, and he is enjoying reading the book of Genesis. God gave us Psalm 25:5, 'Guide me in your truth and teach me, for you are God my Savior, and my hope is in you all day long." He recites this verse nightly. I believe this has brought him closer to Christ. He uses the strategy of throwing the fearful thoughts away in the trash can. He said when he tried to throw them away, his head would hurt. I asked, 'What made them go away?' He smiled and said, 'I know God made them go away.'"

Another Jericho bites the dust.

"Submit yourselves, then, to God. Resist the devil, and he will flee from you" (James 4:7). He will retreat. He *must* retreat. He is not allowed in the place where God is praised. Just keep praising and walking. (From *Glory Days* by Max Lucado.)

REACTION

7. What does this story tell you about the importance of actively resisting the devil?

_____

_____

_____

_____

_____

_____

8. What are some areas in your life where you need God's peace?

_____

_____

_____

_____

_____

9. How can you use the strategy of "throwing the fearful thoughts away in the trash can"?

_____

_____

_____

_____

_____

10. Why do you think believers often try to go it alone instead of relying on God?

_____

_____

_____

_____

11. What are some areas of your life that you find difficult to turn over to God's control? Why?

_____

_____

_____

_____

12. What steps can you take today to draw nearer to God?

_____

_____

_____

_____

LIFE LESSONS

Who do we want to please? The choice is simple for us . . . yet hard. We can please God or someone else (including ourselves). We were created for God's pleasure and glory, but we will sink into petty selfish behavior if we don't humbly bow before God. We can choose friendship with God or friendship with the world. As James shows us in the passage, we can troubleshoot almost any problem we get into by simply asking, "Who am I trying to please?"

DEVOTION

Father, help us to renew our commitment to you—to release all that we have and all that we are to you. We long to give ourselves completely to you so that we might know the freedom available to us only through your grace. Help us to submit ourselves completely to you today.

JOURNALING

How do your actions demonstrate that you are living in complete submission to God?

FOR FURTHER READING

To complete the book of James during this twelve-part study, read James 4:1–10. For more Bible passages on trusting and submitting to God, read Joshua 24:14–15; Psalms 37:4–6; 62:5–8; 143:8–9; Proverbs 3:5–6; Isaiah 25:9; Nahum 1:7; Matthew 6:25–27; and 1 Peter 5:8–9.

SPEAKING WELL OF OTHERS

Do not speak evil of one another, brethren. He who speaks evil of a brother and judges his brother, speaks evil of the law and judges the law. But if you judge the law, you are not a doer of the law but a judge.

JAMES 4:11 NKJV

REFLECTION

As the saying goes, "If you can't say something nice, don't say anything at all." Why do you think this is advice is often so hard to follow? When have your words got you into trouble?

_____

_____

_____

_____

_____

_____

_____

_____

_____

_____

_____

_____

SITUATION

James has just outlined some of the underlying causes of conflict in the congregations that he has been addressing—many of which relate to the issue of *pride*. In this next section of his letter, he continues by focusing specifically on the problem of believers in Christ slandering and judging one another. James was evidently aware that gossiping and lying was taking place in many Christian communities, and he needed to remind the believers that this was not acceptable before God. James also wanted his readers to understand that everything they had came from God—so they had no room to judge others or boast about their own achievements.

OBSERVATION

*Read James 4:11–17 from the New International
Version or the New King James Version.*

NEW INTERNATIONAL VERSION

[11] Brothers and sisters, do not slander one another. Anyone who speaks against a brother or sister or judges them speaks against the law and judges it. When you judge the law, you are not keeping it, but sitting in judgment on it. [12] There is only one Lawgiver and Judge, the one who is able to save and destroy. But you—who are you to judge your neighbor?

[13] Now listen, you who say, "Today or tomorrow we will go to this or that city, spend a year there, carry on business and make money." [14] Why, you do not even know what will happen tomorrow. What is your life? You are a mist that appears for a little while and then vanishes. [15] Instead, you ought to say, "If it is the Lord's will, we will live and do this or that." [16] As it is, you boast in your arrogant schemes. All such boasting is evil. [17] If anyone, then, knows the good they ought to do and doesn't do it, it is sin for them.

NEW KING JAMES VERSION

[11] Do not speak evil of one another, brethren. He who speaks evil of a brother and judges his brother, speaks evil of the law and judges the law. But if you judge the law, you are not a doer of the law but a judge. [12] There is one Lawgiver, who is able to save and to destroy. Who are you to judge another?

[13] Come now, you who say, "Today or tomorrow we will go to such and such a city, spend a year there, buy and sell, and make a profit"; [14] whereas you do not know what will happen tomorrow. For what is your life? It is even a vapor that appears for a little time and then vanishes away. [15] Instead you ought to say, "If the Lord wills, we shall live and do this or that." [16] But now you boast in your arrogance. All such boasting is evil.

[17] Therefore, to him who knows to do good and does not do it, to him it is sin.

EXPLORATION

1. According to James, why should believers in Christ not speak against each other?

2. What does it mean to *slander* another person? How would you define the term?

3. What advice does James offer in this passage about making plans?

4. When does planning turn into boastful pride?

5. What attitude does God want you to have about the future? Why?

_____

_____

_____

_____

_____

6. Why is God not satisfied that you simply _know_ how to do good?

_____

_____

_____

_____

INSPIRATION

I wonder what formed the Grand Canyon.

Maybe a few drips here and there. A leaky underground faucet or a gentle rain on a peaceful night. Slowly more and more water built up. Thunderstorms. Lightning. Angry expressions from the sky spilling out in the raging river called the Colorado.

Soon this river begins to tear through the earth, eating it away, eroding its past. Clawing and ripping. This once-innocent stream now full of power and purpose. As years go by, the crevasse is dug.

Our anger builds like the Colorado. Slowly, slowly small things drip, drip, drip down, annoying, irritating, finally enraging.

That was mine! Drip.

Get out of my way! Drip.

You do this all the time! Drip.

Why can't I get something for once! Drip.

Don't tell me what to do! Drip.

The pressure and the buildup explodes, unleashing a frenzy of anger, pouring out in our words, sweeping away our loved ones, our homes, and our peace.

Don't wait until you have a gushing fire hydrant. Go after the small drips. Address every little irritant with forgiveness and prayer. Slowly the pressure relaxes, and the gauge decreases from ten to four to three, then two and one.

Do it before your anger digs a canyon in your life . . . with you on one side and everyone you know on the other. (From *Max on Life* by Max Lucado.)

REACTION

7. Why is it critical to stop the "drips" when it comes to speaking poorly of others?

_____

_____

_____

_____

8. How have you seen anger and gossip erode relationships in the church?

_____

_____

_____

9. What part does pride play when it comes to judging others and speaking poorly about them?

_____

_____

_____

10. Why do you think it is so hard to practice humility with our words?

_____

_____

_____

_____

11. What have you learned from people in your life who demonstrate a spirit of humility?

_____

_____

_____

12. What steps can you take to develop a spirit of humility as you plan for the future?

_____

_____

_____

LIFE LESSONS

It is easy to fall into the trap of pride—thinking more highly of ourselves than we should—whether that takes the form of judging others with our words or making our own plans without asking God that his will be done. As James notes, "All such boasting is evil" (4:16). This is not to say that we should altogether avoid making plans for the future. Rather, the counsel from James is to prepare for what we can _while_ acknowledging that God is in ultimate control over tomorrow. Looking to him for guidance and affirmation is the best way to keep from being worried about the future or feeling the need to lift ourselves up at the expense of others.

DEVOTION

Father, forgive us for living for ourselves and for thinking that we don't need you. God, help us to embrace humility in our words to others and in our plans for the future. Help us to remember that we can do nothing without you, because you are the source of everything.

JOURNALING

How are you choosing to look to God as your source of affirmation rather than to others?

_____

_____

_____

_____

_____

_____

_____

_____

_____

_____

_____

_____

FOR FURTHER READING

To complete the book of James during this twelve-part study, read James 4:11–17. For more Bible passages on speaking well of others, read Exodus 20:16; Psalm 101:5–7; Proverbs 11:9; Matthew 12:33–37; Colossians 3:5–10; Titus 3:1–2; and 1 Peter 2:1–3.

WARNINGS TO THE RICH

Now listen, you rich people, weep and wail because of the misery that is coming on you. Your wealth has rotted, and moths have eaten your clothes.

JAMES 5:1–2

REFLECTION

In 1 Timothy 6:10, the apostle Paul writes that "the love of money is a root of all kinds of evil." Yet we also know that money can be used for good. Think of a time when you were blessed by the financial generosity of a fellow believer. How did that affect your life?

_____

_____

_____

_____

_____

_____

_____

_____

_____

_____

_____

_____

_____

_____

_____

_____

SITUATION

As previously noted, the recipients of James's letter were likely a mixed group of Jewish and non-Jewish (or Gentile) believers in regions outside of Judea. These believers had come together from widely different backgrounds, status in society, and financial means—a fact that certainly had contributed to the disagreements occurring in their congregations.

In this portion of his letter, James addresses the wealthier members of the community who were not being good stewards of the resources that God had given them ... perhaps the same individuals who were being favored over others in the church. James has bold words about their future plight.

OBSERVATION

Read James 5:1–6 from the New International Version or the New King James Version.

NEW INTERNATIONAL VERSION

[1] Now listen, you rich people, weep and wail because of the misery that is coming on you. [2] Your wealth has rotted, and moths have eaten your clothes. [3] Your gold and silver are corroded. Their corrosion will testify against you and eat your flesh like fire. You have hoarded wealth in the last days. [4] Look! The wages you failed to pay the workers who mowed your fields are crying out against you. The cries of the harvesters have reached the ears of the Lord Almighty. [5] You have lived on earth in luxury and self-indulgence. You have fattened yourselves in the day of slaughter. [6] You have condemned and murdered the innocent one, who was not opposing you.

NEW KING JAMES VERSION

[1] Come now, you rich, weep and howl for your miseries that are coming upon you! [2] Your riches are corrupted, and your garments are moth-eaten. [3] Your gold and silver are corroded, and their corrosion will be a witness against you and will eat your flesh like fire. You have heaped up treasure in the last days. [4] Indeed the wages of the laborers who mowed your fields, which you kept back by fraud, cry out; and the cries of the reapers have reached the ears of the Lord of Sabaoth. [5] You have lived on the earth in pleasure and luxury; you have fattened your hearts as in a day of slaughter. [6] You have condemned, you have murdered the just; he does not resist you.

EXPLORATION

1. What kind of attitude is James addressing with his forceful words in this passage?

_____

_____

_____

_____

_____

2. What were the wealthy people doing in this congregation that drew James's condemnation?

_____

_____

_____

_____

_____

3. How have you seen people oppress others for personal gain?

_____

_____

_____

_____

4. What are some of the ungodly attitudes that cause oppression?

_____

_____

_____

_____

5. How does James say God responds to the oppressed?

_____

_____

_____

_____

6. What are the end results of greed and self-indulgence?

_____

_____

_____

_____

INSPIRATION

We live at one of the great turning points in history. The present division of the world's resources dares not continue. And it will not. Either courageous pioneers will persuade reluctant nations to share the good earth's bounty, or we will enter an era of catastrophic conflict.

Christians should be in the vanguard. The church of Jesus Christ is the most universal body in the world today. All we need to do is truly obey the One we rightly worship. But to obey will mean to follow. And he lives among the poor and oppressed, seeking justice for those in agony. In our time, following in his steps will mean more simple personal lifestyles. It will mean transformed churches . . . costly commitment to structural change in secular society.

Do Christians today have that kind of faith and courage? Will we pioneer new models of sharing for our interdependent world? Will we dare to become the vanguard in the struggle for structural change? . . . I am not pessimistic. God regularly accomplishes his will through faithful remnants. Even in affluent nations, there are millions of Christians who love their Lord Jesus more than houses and lands. More and more Christians are coming to realize that their Lord calls them to feed the hungry and seek justice for the oppressed.

If at this moment in history a few million Christians in affluent nations dare to join hands with the poor around the world, we will decisively influence the course of world history. Together we will strive to be a biblical people ready to follow wherever Scripture leads. We must pray for the courage to bear any cross, suffer any loss, and joyfully embrace any sacrifice that biblical faith requires in an age of hunger. (From *Rich Christians in an Age of Hunger* by Ronald J. Sider.)

REACTION

7. What are some of the *negative* effects that increased wealth can have on people's lives?

_____

_____

_____

_____

8. How can money actually keep believers from doing God's work?

_____

_____

_____

_____

9. How can you use your financial resources for God's glory?

_____

_____

_____

_____

10. Why does it take faith and courage to "pioneer new models of sharing for our interdependent world"? What does that involve?

_____

_____

_____

_____

11. What particular attitudes about money do you feel you need to change?

_____

_____

_____

_____

12. How can sharing the resources God has given to you improve the state of the world?

_____

_____

_____

_____

LIFE LESSONS

Whether or not we consider ourselves among the rich, James's words in this passage can make us feel uncomfortable. In fact . . . they are meant to do so. Whether or not we have what we would consider "sizable" wealth, we tend to base our security on our own resources rather than on God. Anxiety over money—keeping it, growing it, protecting it—can drive us far from our only true security in Christ. And when a wealth-centered life affects the way we treat others, we are on our way to spiritual bankruptcy. James's hard words are merciful warnings.

DEVOTION

Father, keep us from being so blinded by earthly possessions that we fail to see the eternal treasure we cannot lose. Forgive us when we work for greed and gain instead of your glory. Thank you for the blessing of work and for the strength to do it for you.

JOURNALING

How content are you with your financial situation? How has this impacted your attitude?

_____

_____

_____

_____

_____

_____

_____

_____

_____

_____

FOR FURTHER READING

To complete the book of James during this twelve-part study, read James 5:1–6. For more Bible passages on caring for those in need, read Leviticus 23:22; Proverbs 11:28; 23:4; Matthew 19:23–24; Luke 6:23–26; Acts 4:32–35; 1 Timothy 6:9–19; and Hebrews 13:5–6.

LESSON ELEVEN

REWARDS OF PERSEVERANCE

Be patient, brethren, until the coming of the Lord. . . . Establish your hearts, for the coming of the Lord is at hand.
JAMES 5:7–8 NKJV

REFLECTION

James firmly believed that believers in Christ should actively live out their faith. Consider a recent trial or temptation you have faced. How have you been able to persevere with joy in the midst of that difficult situation? What have been the rewards of your perseverance?

SITUATION

James has offered encouragement to those believers in the community who are struggling by reminding them the Lord is aware of their plight—and that he is aware of those who have taken advantage of them. In this next section of his letter, he continues to encourage these believers by pointing to an even greater reason they have to hope: the return of Jesus to the world. James reminds the believers that just as the prophets of old endured in the face of suffering, so can they—and they will be considered blessed for their perseverance. Furthermore, regardless of their present circumstances, they can always count on God's compassion and mercy.

OBSERVATION

Read James 5:7–11 from the New International
Version or the New King James Version.

New International Version

7 Be patient, then, brothers and sisters, until the Lord's coming. See how the farmer waits for the land to yield its valuable crop, patiently waiting for the autumn and spring rains. 8 You too, be patient and stand firm, because the Lord's coming is near. 9 Don't grumble against one another, brothers and sisters, or you will be judged. The Judge is standing at the door!

10 Brothers and sisters, as an example of patience in the face of suffering, take the prophets who spoke in the name of the Lord. 11 As you know, we count as blessed those who have persevered. You have heard of Job's perseverance and have seen what the Lord finally brought about. The Lord is full of compassion and mercy.

New King James Version

7 Therefore be patient, brethren, until the coming of the Lord. See how the farmer waits for the precious fruit of the earth, waiting patiently for

it until it receives the early and latter rain. [8] You also be patient. Establish your hearts, for the coming of the Lord is at hand.

[9] Do not grumble against one another, brethren, lest you be condemned. Behold, the Judge is standing at the door! [10] My brethren, take the prophets, who spoke in the name of the Lord, as an example of suffering and patience. [11] Indeed we count them blessed who endure. You have heard of the perseverance of Job and seen the end intended by the Lord—that the Lord is very compassionate and merciful.

EXPLORATION

1. Why should believers in Christ be motivated to patiently endure?

_____

_____

_____

_____

_____

_____

_____

2. How does the illustration of a farmer demonstrate the importance of patience?

_____

_____

_____

_____

_____

_____

_____

3. Why does James mention grumbling against one another in this passage on patience?

_____

_____

_____

_____

_____

_____

4. Whose example does James say that believers should follow? Why?

_____

_____

_____

_____

_____

_____

5. What did the prophets gain from their suffering?

_____

_____

_____

_____

_____

_____

6. Read Job 42:12–16. How was God's compassion and mercy extended to Job?

_____

_____

_____

_____

_____

INSPIRATION

Julie Lindsey was working the late shift at a hotel just south of Montgomery, Alabama. Her part-time employment helped pay her college bills as she finished school. She was a devout believer. But her belief was tested the night two men held a gun to her head and forced her into their truck. She was robbed, repeatedly raped, and left handcuffed to a tree. It was two o'clock in the morning before she was rescued.

The nightmare nearly destroyed her. She couldn't function, the hotel fired her, and she dropped out of school. In her words, she was "shattered, lost, and bewildered."

This is one of the pieces that doesn't fit the puzzle. How does such a tragedy have a place in God's plan? In time, Julie learned the answer to that question. Listen to her words:

After this experience, I spent a great deal of time thinking about God . . . I searched and I prayed for understanding. I longed to be healed. . . . My spirit and faith were sorely tested, my spiritual journey in the months that followed was painful, but also wonderful. God allowed me to profit from an awful and devastating event. So many good things are in my life now. I have wonderful friends—most of whom I would never have met or known were it not for this experience. I have a job that allows me to work with and serve crime victims. I have a deeper relationship with God. I am spiritually wiser and more mature. I have been blessed, and I am very grateful. . . . Now I ask you, who won?

Julie now has a ministry speaking to groups about God's mercy and healing. Can't you imagine the devil groaning with each message? What he intended for evil, God used for good. Satan unknowingly advanced the cause of the kingdom. Rather than destroy a disciple, he strengthened a disciple.

Think about that the next time evil flaunts its cape and races across your stage. Remember, the final act has already been scripted. And the day Christ comes will be the end of evil. (From *When Christ Comes* by Max Lucado.)

REACTION

7. When has it been difficult for you to persevere as a believer in Christ?

_____

_____

_____

_____

_____

_____

8. How have Christian friends encouraged you to persevere in tough times?

_____

_____

_____

_____

_____

9. How can you pass that encouragement along and help others endure through suffering?

_____

_____

_____

_____

_____

_____

10. How does knowing that Jesus will return give you hope?

_____

_____

_____

_____

_____

11. In what ways have you experienced God's mercy in your life recently?

_____

_____

_____

_____

12. What new insight about God's character have you gained from this lesson?

_____

_____

_____

_____

LIFE LESSONS

Perseverance is an interesting topic of conversation in a Bible study, but it takes on more weight in a setting of pressure, crisis, or tragedy. And we _will_ have troubles. It's not easy to persevere when we need to persevere, but God offers us the assurance of his presence. He reminds us of saints in his Word who have endured far more than we will probably face. And he tells us that no matter what our present circumstances may be, he will have the last word.

DEVOTION

Father, you never promised us this world would be easy or there would be no pain. But you did promise that if we persevere, we would be blessed by your mercy and your grace. Teach us to hold firmly to your promises so that we can endure the struggles and storms of this world.

JOURNALING

How can the promise of Christ's return help you to face your daily struggles?

FOR FURTHER READING

To complete the book of James during this twelve-part study, read James 5:7–11. For more Bible passages on perseverance, read Matthew 24:9–14; Romans 2:7–8; 5:3–4; 8:24–25; 1 Timothy 4:15–16; Hebrews 10:36–38; 12:1–3; and 2 Peter 1:5–9.

LESSON TWELVE

PRAYERS OF FAITH

Therefore confess your sins to each other and pray for each other so that you may be healed. The prayer of a righteous person is powerful and effective.

JAMES 5:16

REFLECTION

From time to time, it's helpful to consider our prayer habits—to reflect on whether we are praying with *faith* or just praying out of *routine*. Take few minutes to think of a time when God answered a specific prayer for you. How did that make you feel? How did it change your life?

_____

_____

_____

_____

_____

_____

_____

_____

_____

_____

_____

SITUATION

James began his letter by encouraging his readers to pray for God's wisdom when they needed it. He now ends his letter with a call for them to pray about *every* situation they face—whether they are in trouble, happy, sick, or in need of forgiveness. James reminds the believers that their prayers will accomplish much in their lives and in the lives of others as they continually rely on God. He urges them to be real and to support one another. As they do this, they will continue the adventure of living out their faith together as the body of Christ.

OBSERVATION

Read James 5:12–20 from the New International Version or the New King James Version.

NEW INTERNATIONAL VERSION

[12] Above all, my brothers and sisters, do not swear—not by heaven or by earth or by anything else. All you need to say is a simple "Yes" or "No." Otherwise you will be condemned.

[13] Is anyone among you in trouble? Let them pray. Is anyone happy? Let them sing songs of praise. [14] Is anyone among you sick? Let them call the elders of the church to pray over them and anoint them with oil in the name of the Lord. [15] And the prayer offered in faith will make the sick person well; the Lord will raise them up. If they have sinned, they will be forgiven. [16] Therefore confess your sins to each other and pray for each other so that you may be healed. The prayer of a righteous person is powerful and effective.

[17] Elijah was a human being, even as we are. He prayed earnestly that it would not rain, and it did not rain on the land for three and a half years. [18] Again he prayed, and the heavens gave rain, and the earth produced its crops.

[19] My brothers and sisters, if one of you should wander from the truth and someone should bring that person back, [20] remember this: Whoever turns a sinner from the error of their way will save them from death and cover over a multitude of sins.

NEW KING JAMES VERSION

[12] But above all, my brethren, do not swear, either by heaven or by earth or with any other oath. But let your "Yes" be "Yes," and your "No," "No," lest you fall into judgment.

[13] Is anyone among you suffering? Let him pray. Is anyone cheerful? Let him sing psalms. [14] Is anyone among you sick? Let him call for the elders of the church, and let them pray over him, anointing him with

117

oil in the name of the Lord. [15] And the prayer of faith will save the sick, and the Lord will raise him up. And if he has committed sins, he will be forgiven. [16] Confess your trespasses to one another, and pray for one another, that you may be healed. The effective, fervent prayer of a righteous man avails much. [17] Elijah was a man with a nature like ours, and he prayed earnestly that it would not rain; and it did not rain on the land for three years and six months. [18] And he prayed again, and the heaven gave rain, and the earth produced its fruit.

[19] Brethren, if anyone among you wanders from the truth, and someone turns him back, [20] let him know that he who turns a sinner from the error of his way will save a soul from death and cover a multitude of sins.

EXPLORATION

1. How would summarize James's final instructions about controlling your speech?

_____

_____

_____

_____

_____

2. What advice does James give to the troubled, the cheerful, and the sick?

_____

_____

_____

_____

_____

3. What steps does James say a believer should take who needs God's healing?

_____

_____

_____

_____

_____

4. What kind of prayer makes great things happen?

_____

_____

_____

_____

5. Read 1 Kings 17:1–4 and 18:41–45. What does Elijah's experience teach you about prayer?

_____

_____

_____

_____

6. What does James say about the importance of guiding those who have fallen into a pattern of sin back to the way of Christ?

_____

_____

_____

_____

INSPIRATION

Computer viruses have had names like Klez, Anna Kournikova, and ILOVEYOU. Mental viruses are known as anxiety, bitterness, anger, guilt, shame, greed, and insecurity. They worm their way into your system and diminish, even disable, your mind. We call these DTPs: destructive thought patterns. (Actually, I'm the only one to call them DTPs.) . . .

If ever there was a DTP candidate, it was George. Abandoned by his father, orphaned by his mother, the little boy was shuffled from foster parent to homelessness and back several times. A sitting duck for bitterness and anger, George could have spent his life getting even. But he didn't. He didn't because Mariah Watkins taught him to think good thoughts.

The needs of each attracted the other—Mariah, a childless washer-woman, and George, a homeless orphan. When Mariah discovered the young boy sleeping in her barn, she took him in. Not only that, she took care of him, took him to church, and helped him find his way to God. When George left Mariah's home, among his few possessions was a Bible she'd given him. By the time he left her home, she had left her mark.

And by the time George left this world, he had left his.

George—George Washington Carver—is a father of modern agri-culture. History credits him with more than three hundred products extracted from peanuts alone. The once-orphaned houseguest of Mariah Watkins became the friend of Henry Ford, Mahatma Gandhi, and three presidents. He entered his laboratory every morning with the prayer, "Open thou mine eyes, that I may behold wondrous things out of thy law."

God answers such prayers. He changes the man by changing the mind. And how does it happen? By doing what you are doing right now. Considering the glory of Christ. "But we all, with unveiled face, behold-ing as in a mirror the glory of the Lord, are being transformed into the same image from glory to glory, just as by the Spirit of the Lord" (2 Corinthians 3:18 NKJV).

To *behold* him is to become like him. As Christ dominates your thoughts, he changes you from one degree of glory to another until—hang on!—you are ready to live with him.

Heaven is the land of sinless minds. Virus-free thinking. Absolute trust. No fear or anger. Shame and second-guessing are practices of a prior life. Heaven will be wonderful, not because the streets are gold, but because our thoughts will be pure.

So what are you waiting for? Apply God's antivirus. "Set your minds on things above, not on things on the earth" (Colossians 3:2 NKJV). Give him your best thoughts, and see if he doesn't change your mind. (From *Next Door Savior* by Max Lucado.)

REACTION

7. What does the story of George Washington Carver tell you about the power of having someone in your life who continually prays for you and points you to God?

_____

_____

_____

_____

_____

_____

8. James says "the prayer of a righteous person is powerful and effective" (verse 16). When have you seen this to be true in your life?

_____

_____

_____

_____

_____

9. James states that Elijah was human, "even as we are" (verse 17). How does this encourage you when it comes to praying for God to do great things in your life?

_____
_____
_____
_____
_____

10. What great things would you like to see God do in your life or the lives of others?

_____
_____
_____
_____
_____

11. What commitment are you willing to make to pray for those things?

_____
_____
_____
_____
_____

12. How can you develop more discipline and patience in your daily prayer life?

_____
_____
_____
_____
_____

LIFE LESSONS

Prayer should be the default setting for a Christian's life. Paul instructed us to "pray without ceasing" (1 Thessalonians 5:17 NKJV), and James would have concurred. What begins as a conscious and deliberate habit can become, over time, a way of living that maintains constant contact with God. The challenges of life and the needs of other people become opportunities to bring to the forefront the prayer life that is going on in the background of our minds continuously. That is the effective prayer life that avails much!

DEVOTION

Father, we cherish your promise to answer our prayers. Yet we often come to you with muddled ideas, unsure of what is best, uncertain of your will, and unwilling to wait for your answers. We thank you for your assurance that our imperfect prayers cannot hinder your incredible power.

JOURNALING

What is a situation that is troubling you right now? Write a prayer to God about it below.

FOR FURTHER READING

To complete the book of James during this twelve-part study, read James 5:12–20. For more Bible passages on prayer, read Psalm 6:8–10; Proverbs 15:8; Jeremiah 33:2–3; Matthew 6:5–8; John 15:5–8; Romans 8:26–27; Ephesians 6:18–20; Philippians 4:6–7; and Colossians 4:2–6.

LEADER'S GUIDE FOR SMALL GROUPS

Thank you for your willingness to lead a group through *Life Lessons from James*. The rewards of being a leader are different from those of participating, and we hope you find your own walk with Jesus deepened by this experience. During the twelve lessons in this study, you will guide your group through selected passages in James and explore the key themes of the letter. There are several elements in this leader's guide that will help you as you structure your study and reflection time, so be sure to follow along and take advantage of each one.

BEFORE YOU BEGIN

Before your first meeting, make sure the group members have their own copy of the *Life Lessons from James* study guide so they can follow along and have their answers written out ahead of time. Alternately, you can hand out the guides at your first meeting and give the group some time to look over the material and ask any preliminary questions. Be sure to send a sheet around the room during that first meeting and have the members write down their name, phone number, and email address so you can keep in touch with them during the week.

There are two ways to structure the duration of the study. You can choose to cover each lesson individually for a total of twelve weeks of discussion, or you can combine two lessons together per week for a total of six weeks of discussion. (Note that if the group members read the selected passages of Scripture for each lesson, they will cover the entire book of James during the study.) The following table illustrates these options:

Twelve-Week Format

Week	Lessons Covered	Reading
1	Growing Through Trials	James 1:1–11
2	Enduring Temptation	James 1:12–18
3	Listening and Doing	James 1:19–27
4	Equality in the Church	James 2:1–13
5	How Faith Works	James 2:14–26
6	Taming the Tongue	James 3:1–12
7	Sowing Seeds of Peace	James 3:13–18
8	Submitting to God	James 4:1–10
9	Speaking Well of Others	James 4:11–17
10	Warnings to the Rich	James 5:1–6
11	Rewards of Perseverance	James 5:7–11
12	Prayers of Faith	James 5:12–20

Six-Week Format

Week	Lessons Covered	Reading
1	Growing Through Trials / Enduring Temptation	James 1:1–18
2	Listening and Doing / Equality in the Church	James 1:19–2:13
3	How Faith Works / Taming the Tongue	James 2:14–3:12
4	Sowing Seeds of Peace / Submitting to God	James 3:13–4:10
5	Speaking Well of Others / Warnings to the Rich	James 4:11–5:6
6	Rewards of Perseverance / Prayers of Faith	James 5:7–20

Generally, the ideal size you will want for the group is between eight to ten people, which ensures everyone will have enough time to participate in discussions. If you have more people, you might want to break up the main group into smaller subgroups. Encourage those who show up at the first meeting to commit to attending the duration of the study, as this will help the group members get to know each other, create stability for the group, and help you know how to prepare each week.

Each of the lessons begins with a brief reflection that highlights the theme you will be discussing that week. As you begin your group time, have the group members briefly respond to the opening question to get them thinking about the topic at hand. Some people may want to tell a long story in response to one of these questions, but the goal is to keep the answers brief. Ideally, you want everyone in the group to get a chance to answer, so try to keep the responses to just a few minutes. If you have more talkative group members, say up front that everyone needs to limit his or her answer to two minutes.

Give the group members a chance to answer, but tell them to feel free to pass if they wish. With the rest of the study, it's generally not a good idea to have everyone answer every question—a free-flowing discussion is more desirable. But with the opening reflection question, you can go around the circle. Encourage shy people to share, but don't force them.

Before your first meeting, let the group members know how the lessons are broken down. During your group discussion time the members will be drawing on the answers they wrote to the Exploration and Reaction sections, so encourage them to always complete these ahead of time. Also, invite them to bring any questions and insights they uncovered while reading to your next meeting, especially if they had a breakthrough moment or if they didn't understand something they read.

WEEKLY PREPARATION

As the leader, there are a few things you should do to prepare for each meeting:

- *Read through the lesson.* This will help you to become familiar with the content and know how to structure the discussion times.
- *Decide which questions you want to discuss.* Depending on how you structure your group time, you may not be able to cover every

question. So select the questions ahead of time that you absolutely want the group to explore.

- *Be familiar with the questions you want to discuss.* When the group meets you'll be watching the clock, so you want to make sure you are familiar with the Bible study questions you have selected. You can then spend time in the passage again when the group meets. In this way, you'll ensure you have the passage more deeply in your mind than your group members.
- *Pray for your group.* Pray for your group members throughout the week and ask God to lead them as they study his Word.
- *Bring extra supplies to your meeting.* The members should bring their own pens for writing notes, but it's a good idea to have extras available for those who forget. You may also want to bring paper and additional Bibles.

Note that in many cases there will not be one "right" answer to the question. Answers will vary, especially when the group members are being asked to share their personal experiences.

STRUCTURING THE DISCUSSION TIME

You will need to determine with your group how long you want to meet each week so you can plan your time accordingly. Generally, most groups like to meet for either sixty minutes or ninety minutes, so you could use one of the following schedules:

Section	60 Minutes	90 Minutes
WELCOME (members arrive and get settled)	5 minutes	10 minutes
REFLECTION (discuss the opening question for the lesson)	10 minutes	15 minutes
DISCUSSION (discuss the Bible study questions in the Exploration and Reaction sections)	35 minutes	50 minutes
PRAYER/CLOSING (pray together as a group and dismiss)	10 minutes	15 minutes

As the group leader, it is up to you to keep track of the time and keep things moving along according to your schedule. You might want to set a timer for each segment so both you and the group members know when your time is up. (Note that there are some good phone apps for timers that play a gentle chime or other pleasant sound instead of a disruptive noise.) Don't feel pressured to cover every question you have selected if the group has a good discussion going. Again, it's not necessary to go around the circle and make everyone share.

Don't be concerned if the group members are silent or slow to share. People are often quiet when they are pulling together their ideas, and this might be a new experience for them. Just ask a question and let it hang in the air until someone shares. You can then say, "Thank you. What about others? What came to you when you reflected on the passage?"

GROUP DYNAMICS

Leading a group through *Life Lessons from James* will prove to be highly rewarding both to you and your group members—but that doesn't mean you will not encounter any challenges along the way! Discussions can get off track. Group members may not be sensitive to the needs and ideas of others. Some might worry they will be expected to talk about matters that make them feel awkward. Others may express comments that result in disagreements. To help ease this strain on you and the group, consider the following ground rules:

- When someone raises a question or comment that is off the main topic, suggest you deal with it another time, or, if you feel led to go in that direction, let the group know you will be spending some time discussing it.
- If someone asks a question you don't know how to answer, admit it and move on. At your discretion, feel free to invite group members to comment on questions that call for personal experience.

- If you find one or two people are dominating the discussion time, direct a few questions to others in the group. Outside the main group time, ask the more dominating members to help you draw out the quieter ones. Work to make them a part of the solution instead of the problem.
- When a disagreement occurs, encourage the group members to process the matter in love. Encourage those on opposite sides to restate what they heard the other side say about the matter, and then invite each side to evaluate if that perception is accurate. Lead the group in examining other Scriptures related to the topic and look for common ground.

When any of these issues arise, encourage your group members to follow the words from the Bible: "Love one another" (John 13:34), "If it is possible, as far as it depends on you, live at peace with everyone" (Romans 12:18), and, "Be quick to listen, slow to speak and slow to become angry" (James 1:19).

Thank you again for taking the time to lead your group. May God reward your efforts and dedication and make your time together in this study fruitful for his kingdom.

ALSO AVAILABLE IN THE LIFE LESSONS SERIES

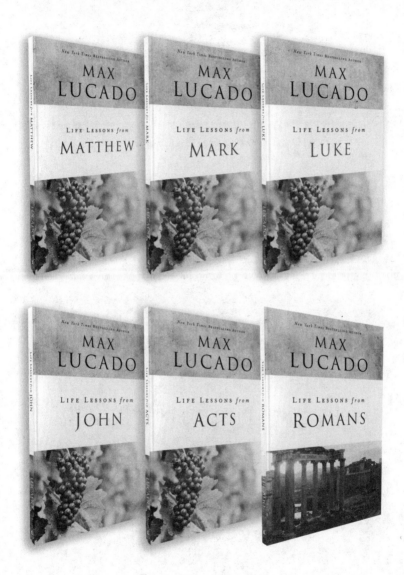

Now available wherever books and ebooks are sold.

ALSO AVAILABLE IN THE LIFE LESSONS SERIES

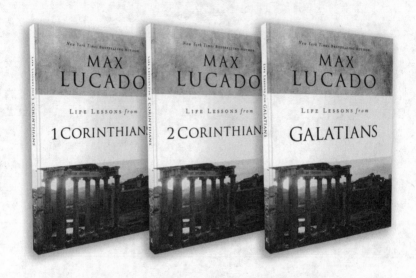

Now available wherever books and ebooks are sold.